Essential Guide to Writing

Writing Avenue

Rachel Somer

Paragraph Writing

2

 DARAKWON

About the Author

Rachel Somer

BA in English Literature, York University, Toronto, Canada

Award-winning essayist, TOEIC developer, and author of educational books

Over ten years of experience as an English as a Second Language instructor

The author of *Fundamental Reading* Basic 1 and 2

--------- **Essential Guide to Writing** ---------

Writing Avenue 2
Paragraph Writing

Publisher Chung Kyudo
Author Rachel Somer
Editors Jeong Yeonsoon, Kim Mina, Seo Jeong-ah, Kim Mikyeong
Designers Park Narae, Forest

First published in February 2021
By Darakwon, Inc.
Darakwon Bldg., 211, Munbal-ro, Paju-si, Gyeonggi-do 10881
Republic of Korea
Tel: 82-2-736-2031 (Ext. 250)
Fax: 82-2-732-2037

ISBN 978-89-277-0448-5 54740
978-89-277-0446-1 54740 (set)

www.darakwon.co.kr

Photo Credits
Muhammad Anuar bin Jamal (p. 14), arda savasciogullari (p. 34),
Sveta Imnadze (p. 72), NAZRUL NAIM BIN NAZMI (p. 82),
chingyunsong (p. 84), Sarunyu L (p. 84), Michael San Diego (p. 84),
Anton_Ivanov (p. 84), Alexander Tolstykh (p. 84), Craig Russell (p. 87) /
www.shutterstock.com

Components Main Book / Workbook
11 10 9 8 7 6 5   24 25 26 27 28

Essential Guide to Writing

Writing Avenue

Paragraph Writing

2

Table of Contents

Unit	Topic	Writing Goal	Type of Writing
Unit 1	**My Dream Job**	Write about your dream job.	Expository Writing » Presentation
Unit 2	My Weekend	Write about what you do on the weekend.	Narrative Writing » Journal
Unit 3	**My Special Birthday Gift**	Write about a special birthday gift you received.	Narrative Writing » Journal
Unit 4	My Favorite Teacher	Write about your favorite teacher.	Narrative Writing » Letter
Unit 5	**Follow the Rules**	Write about the rules at a public place.	Expository Writing » Report
Unit 6	A Famous Food	Write about a famous food.	Descriptive Writing » Poster
Unit 7	**The Best Place in My Town**	Write about the best place in your town.	Descriptive Writing » Blog
Unit 8	My Favorite Movie	Write about your favorite movie.	Expository Writing » Movie Review

How to Use This Book

• Student Book

1. Before You Write

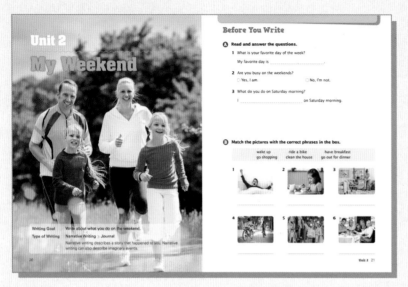

Thinking about the Topic

Three warm-up questions help students think about the writing topic.

Previewing the Key Vocabulary

Students can learn the key vocabulary by matching the words with the pictures or filling in the table.

2. Understanding the Model Text

QR code for listening to the model text

Reading the Model Text

Students can read an example of the writing topic and use it as a template when they write their passage.

Completing the Graphic Organizer

By completing the graphic organizer, students can learn the structure of the model text. This also helps them organize their writing.

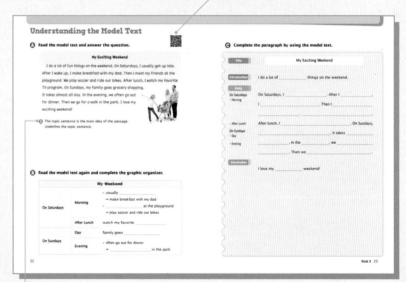

A question about the model text is provided.

Completing the Paragraph

By completing the paragraph, students can review the model text and learn what the passage consists of.

3. Collecting Ideas

Getting Ideas from Collecting Ideas

Ideas related to the writing topic are provided. Students can brainstorm and learn new ideas before writing their draft.

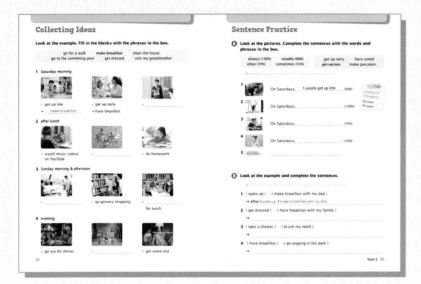

4. Sentence Practice

Practicing Sentences with Key Structures

Various types of questions allow students to practice the key structures of the model text. They also help students gather ideas before writing.

5. Sentence Practice Plus

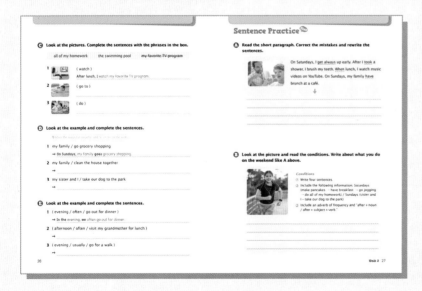

Correcting a Short Paragraph

Students can check if they understand the key structures they learned by correcting the mistakes in the short paragraph.

Writing a Short Paragraph

Students should write a short paragraph by using the given picture and the conditions. This helps students practice the key structures.

6. Brainstorming & First Draft

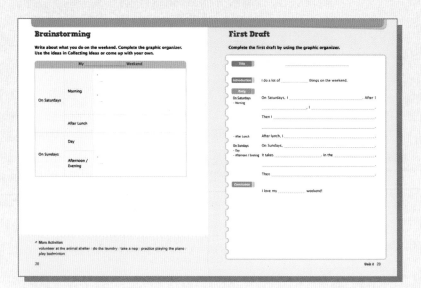

Brainstorming

By completing the graphic organizer, students can organize their ideas prior to writing the first draft.

First Draft

Students should complete the first draft by using the graphic organizer. They can revise, edit the first draft, and write the final draft in the workbook.

Vocabulary and Structure Review

Students can review the key vocabulary they learned in each unit by writing the meaning of each word and phrase. They can also review the key structures in the unit.

• Workbook

7. More Questions

Students can practice and review the key structures. They can also complete the model text by matching the phrases.

8. Revise & Edit ➜ Final Draft

After writing the first draft, students can revise and edit the draft, and then write the final draft.

About Paragraph Writing

1. What Is a Paragraph?

A paragraph is a short piece of writing that handles a single idea or concept. All the sentences in a given paragraph should be related to a single topic. Paragraphs can stand alone, or they can be added to longer pieces of writing such as essays, stories, articles, and many more.

2. What Does a Paragraph Consist of?

A paragraph consists of a topic sentence, supporting details, and a concluding sentence.

– The topic sentence is the main idea of the passage.

– Supporting details are information and examples that explain the topic.

– The concluding sentence is the final thought of the passage.

Topic sentence   **My Exciting Weekend**   Supporting details

I do a lot of fun things on the weekend. On Saturdays, I usually get up late. After I wake up, I make breakfast with my dad. Then I meet my friends at the playground. We play soccer and ride our bikes. After lunch, I watch my favorite TV program. On Sundays, my family goes grocery shopping. It takes almost all day. In the evening, we often go out for dinner. Then we go for a walk in the park. I love my exciting weekend!

Concluding sentence

3. What Are the Types of Paragraph Writing?

1) Expository Writing

It gives information about a topic or tells you how to do something.

2) Narrative Writing

It describes a story that happened to you. It can also describe imaginary events.

3) Persuasive Writing

It encourages a reader to make a choice by providing evidence and examples.

4) Descriptive Writing

It describes a person, place, or thing. It shows what the person, location, or object is like.

Unit 1
My Dream Job

Writing Goal	Write about your dream job.
Type of Writing	Expository Writing » Presentation
	Expository writing gives information about a topic or tells you how to do something.

Before You Write

A Read and answer the questions.

1 Do you have a dream job?

☐ Yes, I do.   ☐ No, I don't.

2 Do you want to go to college?

☐ Yes, I do.   ☐ No, I don't.

3 What do you want to be when you grow up?

I want to be a(n) _____ .

B Match the pictures with the correct words in the box.

doctor   architect   vet
pilot   animator   florist

1

_____

2

_____

3

_____

4

_____

5

_____

6

_____

Understanding the Model Text

A **Read the model text and answer the question.**

I Want to Be a Pilot

I want to be a pilot when I grow up. Pilots work on airplanes. They fly the planes from one place to another. I like this job because I love to travel. I will visit many countries when I am a pilot. Pilots need to be smart and responsible. They also need to know a lot about airplanes. It is a difficult job, so I need to prepare. I will go to a flight school and study hard. I think I will be a great pilot someday!

Q The topic sentence is the main idea of the passage. Underline the topic sentence.

B **Read the model text again and complete the graphic organizer.**

I Want to Be a Pilot	
What Pilots Do	• work on _____ • _____ from one place to another
Why I Like This Job	• love _____ → will visit many _____
What Pilots Need to Do	• be smart and _____ • _____ a lot about airplanes
What I Need to Do	• go to _____ • study hard

C Complete the paragraph by using the model text.

Title	I Want to Be a Pilot

Introduction

I want to be _____ I grow up.

Body

What Pilots Do

_____ work _____. They _____

Why I Like This Job

_____. I like this job because I _____

_____. I will _____ when I am

What Pilots Need to Do

_____. _____ need to be _____

_____. They also need _____

a lot about _____. It is a _____ job,

What I Need to Do

so I need to _____. I will _____

and _____.

Conclusion

I think I will be a great _____ someday!

Collecting Ideas

Look at the example. Fill in the blanks with the phrases in the box.

animated films	grow flowers	~~love to travel~~
cure many patients	look at beautiful buildings	take care of sick pets

1
pilot

- _love to travel_
- visit many countries

2
vet

- really like animals
- _____

  and zoo animals

3
architect

- love to _____
- design amazing buildings

4
doctor

- like to help sick people
- _____

5
florist

- like to _____
- make beautiful flower bouquets

6
animator

- love to draw cartoons
- work on _____

Sentence Practice

A **Look at the pictures. Complete the sentences with the words and phrases in the box.**

~~fly~~	draw	sick animals	cartoon characters
design	take care of	~~the planes~~	many kinds of buildings

1 They _____ fly the planes _____ from one place to another.

2 They _____.

3 They _____.

4 They _____.

B **Look at the example and rewrite the sentences.**

I like this job. I love to travel.

→ I like this job **because** I love to travel.

Use "because" to give a reason.

1 I like this job. I really like animals.

→ _____

2 I like this job. I like to grow flowers.

→ _____

3 I like this job. I love to look at beautiful buildings.

→ _____

Your Idea

4 _____

C **Look at the example and rewrite the sentences.**

💡 In time clause with "when," use present tense for future actions.

1 I am a pilot. I will visit many countries.

→ I will visit many countries **when** I am a pilot.

2 I am a vet. I will take care of sick pets and zoo animals.

→ _____

3 I am an architect. I will design amazing buildings.

→ _____

D **Look at the pictures and complete the sentences.**

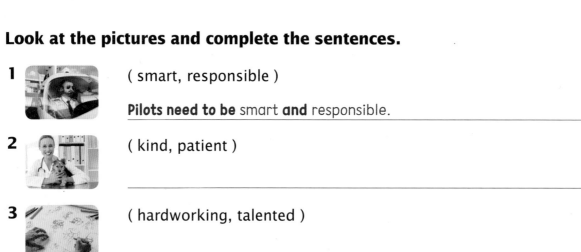

1 (smart, responsible)

Pilots need to be smart **and** responsible.

2 (kind, patient)

_____

3 (hardworking, talented)

_____

E **Look at the example and complete the sentences.**

1 (go to a flight school / study hard)

→ **I will** go to a flight school **and** study hard.

2 (study hard / learn about animals)

→ _____

3 (go to a medical school / learn about the body)

→ _____

Sentence Practice Plus

A **Read the short paragraph. Correct the mistakes and rewrite the sentences.**

I want to be an animator when I <u>grow</u>. They <u>drawing</u> cartoon characters. I like this job <u>so</u> I love to draw cartoons. I will work on animated films <u>while</u> I am an animator.

_____

_____

_____

_____

B **Look at the picture and read the conditions. Write about your dream job like A above.**

Conditions
① Write four sentences.
② Include the following information: help sick people / like to help sick people / cure many patients.
③ Include "when" and "because."

_____

_____

_____

_____

Brainstorming

Write about your dream job. Complete the graphic organizer. Use the ideas in Collecting Ideas or come up with your own.

I Want to Be _____	
What _____ **Do**	• •
Why I Like This Job	• →
What _____ **Need to Do**	• •
What I Need to Do	• •

More Jobs

photographer / judge / actor / computer programmer / fashion designer / inventor

First Draft

Complete the first draft by using the graphic organizer.

Title	_____
Introduction	I want to be _____ I grow up.
Body	
What They Do	_____ work _____.
Why I Like This Job	They _____. I like this job because I _____. I will _____ _____ when I _____.
What They Need to Do	_____ need to be _____. They also need _____ a lot about _____.
What I Need to Do	It is _____ job, so I need to _____. I will _____ and _____.
Conclusion	I think I will be _____ someday!

Unit 2
My Weekend

Writing Goal	Write about what you do on the weekend.
Type of Writing	Narrative Writing » Journal
	Narrative writing describes a story that happened to you. Narrative writing can also describe imaginary events.

Before You Write

A **Read and answer the questions.**

1 What is your favorite day of the week?

My favorite day is _____.

2 Are you busy on the weekends?

☐ Yes, I am.   ☐ No, I'm not.

3 What do you do on Saturday morning?

I _____ on Saturday morning.

B **Match the pictures with the correct phrases in the box.**

wake up	ride a bike	have breakfast
go shopping	clean the house	go out for dinner

1

_____

2

_____

3

_____

4

_____

5

_____

6

_____

Understanding the Model Text

A **Read the model text and answer the question.**

My Exciting Weekend

I do a lot of fun things on the weekend. On Saturdays, I usually get up late. After I wake up, I make breakfast with my dad. Then I meet my friends at the playground. We play soccer and ride our bikes. After lunch, I watch my favorite TV program. On Sundays, my family goes grocery shopping. It takes almost all day. In the evening, we often go out for dinner. Then we go for a walk in the park. I love my exciting weekend!

Q The topic sentence is the main idea of the passage. Underline the topic sentence.

B **Read the model text again and complete the graphic organizer.**

My Weekend		
On Saturdays	**Morning**	• usually _____ → make breakfast with my dad • _____ at the playground → play soccer and ride our bikes
	After Lunch	watch my favorite _____
On Sundays	**Day**	family goes _____
	Evening	• often go out for dinner → _____ in the park

C **Complete the paragraph by using the model text.**

My Exciting Weekend

Introduction

I do a lot of _____ things on the weekend.

Body

On Saturdays
- Morning

On Saturdays, I _____. After I _____,

I _____. Then I _____

_____. _____.

- After Lunch

After lunch, I _____. On Sundays,

On Sundays
- Day

_____. It takes _____

- Evening

_____. In the _____, we _____

_____. Then we _____.

Conclusion

I love my _____ weekend!

Collecting Ideas

Look at the example. Fill in the blanks with the phrases in the box.

go for a walk	~~make breakfast~~	clean the house
go to the swimming pool	get dressed	visit my grandmother

1 Saturday morning

- get up late
→   make breakfast

- get up early
→ have breakfast

- _____

2 after lunch

- watch music videos on YouTube

- _____

- do homework

3 Sunday morning & afternoon

- _____

- go grocery shopping

- _____ for lunch

4 evening

- go out for dinner

- _____

- get some rest

Sentence Practice

A Look at the pictures. Complete the sentences with the words and phrases in the box.

always (100%) ~~usually (90%)~~	get up early have cereal
often (70%) sometimes (50%)	~~get up late~~ make pancakes

🔔 Remember to place an adverb of frequency before the main verb.

1 On Saturdays, <u>I usually get up late</u>. (90%)

+TIP

Adverbs of Frequency

5% rarely
0% never

2 On Saturdays, _____. (100%)

3 On Saturdays, _____. (70%)

4 On Saturdays, _____. (50%)

5 Your Idea   _____

B Look at the example and complete the sentences.

🔔 When "after" is used as a conjunction, it is followed by a subject and a verb.

1 (wake up) → (make breakfast with my dad)

→ **After I** wake up, **I** make breakfast with my dad.

2 (get dressed) → (have breakfast with my family)

→ _____

3 (take a shower) → (brush my teeth)

→ _____

4 (have breakfast) → (go jogging in the park)

→ _____

C Look at the pictures. Complete the sentences with the phrases in the box.

all of my homework	the swimming pool	~~my favorite TV program~~

1 (watch)

After lunch, I watch my favorite TV program.

2 (go to)

_____

3 (do)

_____

D Look at the example and complete the sentences.

💡 When the subject is singular, add "s" or "es" to the verb.

1 my family / go grocery shopping

➡ **On Sundays,** my family **goes** grocery shopping.

2 my family / clean the house together

➡ _____

3 my sister and I / take our dog to the park

➡ _____

E Look at the example and complete the sentences.

1 (evening / often / go out for dinner)

➡ **In the** evening, **we** often go out for dinner.

2 (afternoon / often / visit my grandmother for lunch)

➡ _____

3 (evening / usually / go for a walk)

➡ _____

Sentence Practice Plus

A **Read the short paragraph. Correct the mistakes and rewrite the sentences.**

On Saturdays, I <u>get always</u> up early. After I <u>took</u> a shower, I brush my teeth. <u>When</u> lunch, I watch music videos on YouTube. On Sundays, my family <u>have</u> brunch at a café.

_____

_____

_____

_____

B **Look at the picture and read the conditions. Write about what you do on the weekend like A above.**

Conditions

① Write four sentences.

② Include the following information: Saturdays (make pancakes → have breakfast → go jogging → do all of my homework) / Sundays (sister and I – take our dog to the park)

② Include an adverb of frequency and "after + noun / after + subject + verb."

_____

_____

_____

_____

Brainstorming

Write about what you do on the weekend. Complete the graphic organizer. Use the ideas in Collecting Ideas or come up with your own.

My _____ Weekend		
On Saturdays	Morning	• → • →
	After Lunch	
On Sundays	Day	
	Afternoon / Evening	• →

◆ More Activities

volunteer at the animal shelter / do the laundry / take a nap / practice playing the piano / play badminton

First Draft

Complete the first draft by using the graphic organizer.

Title	_____
Introduction	I do a lot of _____ things on the weekend.
Body	
On Saturdays - Morning	On Saturdays, I _____. After I _____, I _____. Then I _____. _____.
- After Lunch	After lunch, I _____.
On Sundays - Day - Afternoon / Evening	On Sundays, _____. It takes _____. In the _____, _____. Then _____.
Conclusion	I love my _____ weekend!

Unit 3

My Special Birthday Gift

Writing Goal	Write about a special birthday gift you received.
Type of Writing	Narrative Writing » Journal
	Narrative writing describes a story that happened to you. Narrative writing can also describe imaginary events.

Before You Write

A **Read and answer the questions.**

1 When is your birthday?

My birthday is on _____ .

2 Do you like birthday parties?

☐ Yes, I do.   ☐ No, I don't.

3 What do you do on your birthday?

I _____ on my birthday.

B **Match the pictures with the correct words and phrases in the box.**

| puppy | diary | model car |
| scarf | bracelet | cell phone case |

1

_____

2

_____

3

_____

4

_____

5

_____

6

_____

Understanding the Model Text

A **Read the model text and answer the question.**

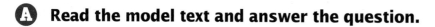

My Special Bracelet

My birthday is on April 10. Every year, I have a birthday party. My friends come to my house. We eat cake together, and then I open gifts. Last year, my best friend gave me a special gift. It was inside a pink box. I opened the box and saw a beautiful bracelet. It is silver with colorful hearts on it. I thought it was so pretty! I wear my bracelet every day. It reminds me of my best friend. I hope I never lose my special bracelet.

Q The concluding sentence is the final thought of the passage. Underline the concluding sentence.

B **Read the model text again and complete the graphic organizer.**

My Bracelet	
My Birthday	on _____
What I Do at My Birthday Party	• _____ come to my house • eat cake together • _____
My Special Gift	• Who Gave It to Me: _____ • What It Is: a beautiful _____ • What It Looks Like: silver with _____ on it • wear my bracelet every day

C Complete the paragraph by using the model text.

| Title | My Special Bracelet |

Introduction
My Birthday

My birthday is on _____.

Body

What I Do at My
Birthday Party

Every year, I have a birthday party. My _____

_____. We _____, and then I open gifts.

My Special Gift
- Who Gave It to Me

_____, _____ gave

_____ a special gift. It was _____.

- What It Is

I opened _____ and saw _____.

- What It Looks Like

It is _____. I thought

it _____! I _____ every day.

It reminds me of _____.

Conclusion

I hope I never lose _____.

Collecting Ideas

Look at the example. Fill in the blanks with the phrases in the box.

white polka dots	play with my puppy	~~colorful hearts~~
black with spaceships	work on my model car	write in my diary

1

- a beautiful bracelet
- silver with _colorful hearts_ on it
- wear my bracelet every day

2

- a new diary
- blue with a silver star on it
- _____ every day

3

- a warm scarf
- red with _____ on it
- wear my scarf every day

4

- a model car
- yellow with black stripes on it
- _____ every day

5

- a new cell phone case
- _____ on it
- use my cell phone case every day

6

- a little puppy
- white with brown spots on it
- _____ every day

Sentence Practice

A **Look at the example and rewrite the sentences.**

I got a special gift from my best friend.
→ My best friend **gave me** a special gift.

💡 "Give" is followed by an indirect object (a person) and a direct object (a thing).

1 I got a special gift from my aunt.

→ _____

2 I got a special gift from my parents.

→ _____

3 I got a special gift from my cousin.

→ _____

Your Idea

4 _____

B **Look at the pictures. Complete the sentences with the phrases in the box.**

a new diary	~~a beautiful bracelet~~
a little puppy	a new cell phone case

1 (the box)

→ **I opened** the box **and saw** a beautiful bracelet. _____

2 (the bag)

→ _____

3 (the bag)

→ _____

4 (the box)

→ _____

5 Your Idea _____

C Look at the pictures. Complete the sentences with the words and phrases in the box.

~~silver~~   blue   red   a silver star   white polka dots   ~~colorful hearts~~

1 It is silver **with** colorful hearts **on it**.

2 _____

3 _____

D Look at the example and rewrite the sentences.

1 It is so pretty!   → **I thought** it **was** so pretty!

2 It is so nice!   → _____

3 It is so cute!   → _____

E Look at the pictures. Complete the sentences with the phrases in the box.

write in my diary   ~~wear my bracelet~~
work on my model car

1 I wear my bracelet **every day**.

2 _____

3 _____

Sentence Practice Plus

A **Read the short paragraph. Correct the mistakes and rewrite the sentences.**

Last year, my parents gave <u>my</u> a special gift. I <u>open</u> the box and saw a little puppy. It is white with brown spots on it. I thought it <u>is</u> so cute! I <u>playing</u> with my puppy every day.

_____

_____

_____

_____

B **Look at the picture and read the conditions. Write about your special gift like A above.**

Conditions

① Write five sentences.

② Include the following information: grandmother / warm scarf / soft / wear my scarf.

③ Include the past tense and "give + indirect object + direct object."

_____

_____

_____

_____

Brainstorming

Write about a special birthday gift you received. Complete the graphic organizer. Use the ideas in Collecting Ideas or come up with your own.

My Special _____	
My Birthday	
What I Do at My Birthday Party	• • •
My Special Gift	• Who Gave It to Me: • What It Is: • What It Looks Like: •

◆ **More Special Gifts**

a cool game console / a furry kitten / a new bike / a baseball cap

First Draft

Complete the first draft by using the graphic organizer.

Title _____

Introduction

My Birthday

My birthday is on _____.

Body

What I Do at My Birthday Party

Every year, I have a birthday party. My _____

_____. We _____, and then

My Special Gift
- Who Gave It to Me

I open gifts. _____, _____ gave

_____ a special gift. It was _____.

- What It Is

I opened _____ and saw _____ ____.

- What It Looks Like

It is _____. I thought it

_____! I _____ every day.

It reminds me of _____.

Conclusion

I hope I never lose _____.

Unit 4
My Favorite Teacher

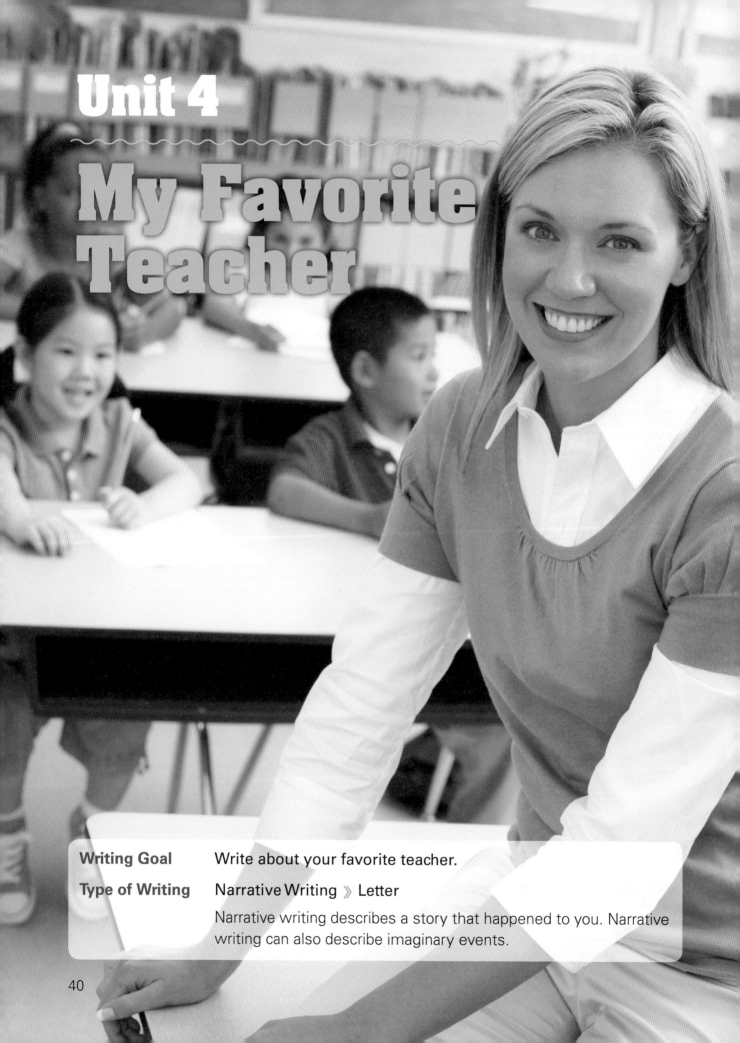

Writing Goal	Write about your favorite teacher.
Type of Writing	Narrative Writing » Letter
	Narrative writing describes a story that happened to you. Narrative writing can also describe imaginary events.

Before You Write

A **Read and answer the questions.**

1 What grade are you in?

I am in _____ .

2 Who is your favorite teacher?

My favorite teacher is _____ .

3 What subject does he / she teach?

He / She teaches _____ .

B **Fill in the chart with the words in the box.**

cheerful	exciting	friendly	tiring
patient	interesting	difficult	enthusiastic

The subject is ...	The teacher is ...
• _____	• _____
• _____	• _____
• _____	• _____
• _____	• _____

Understanding the Model Text

A **Read the model text and answer the question.**

Thank You, Miss Bell

Dear Jenny,

Do you remember Miss Bell? She was our fourth-grade teacher. She was tall and thin. She had curly brown hair and freckles. She taught us math. I always thought math was difficult. But Miss Bell was patient and never scolded us. Because of her, my math scores improved. She made math fun! Now, we are in middle school. Math is easier than other subjects. I really want to thank Miss Bell for teaching us.

Your friend,

Mary

Q What is the passage mainly about?
   a. Mary's favorite teacher
   b. Jenny's music teacher

B **Read the model text again and complete the graphic organizer.**

Miss Bell	
Who	_____ math teacher
Appearance	• tall and _____ • curly brown hair and _____
Personality	• patient • never _____
Why I Am Thankful	• thought math was _____ → math scores _____ → made math fun • math is _____ than other subjects

C Complete the paragraph by using the model text.

Title	Thank You, Miss Bell

Introduction

Dear _____,

Body

Who

Do you remember _____? She was our _____

Appearance

teacher. _____ was _____. _____

had _____. _____

taught us _____. I always thought _____

Personality

was _____. But _____ was _____

Why I Am Thankful

and _____. Because of _____, _____

_____. _____ made _____!

Now, we are _____. _____ is _____

than other subjects. I really want to thank _____

for teaching us.

Conclusion

Your friend,

_____

Collecting Ideas

Look at the example. Fill in the blanks with the phrases in the box.

~~math scores improved~~	reading skills improved	become a doctor
interested in society	play the guitar	soccer skills improved

1

- math teacher: patient

→ _math scores improved_

2

- P.E. teacher: enthusiastic

→ basketball and

_____

3

- social studies teacher: cheerful

→ became _____

4

- music teacher: funny

→ learned to

_____

5

- English teacher: kind

→ _____

6

- science teacher: friendly

→ want to _____

Sentence Practice

(A) Look at the example and complete the sentences.

> (she / tall / thin) (curly brown hair / freckles)
> → She **was** tall **and** thin. She **had** curly brown hair **and** freckles.

💡 Use "be verbs" when describing someone's entire body. Use "have" when describing a feature.

1 (he / tall / strong) (black hair / bright green eyes)

→ _____

2 (she / short / skinny) (short hair / pink glasses)

→ _____

3 (he / tall / thin) (wavy hair / a beard)

→ _____

Your Idea

4 _____

(B) Look at the example and complete the sentences.

> Miss Bell / patient / scold us
> → Miss Bell **was** patient **and never scolded** us.

1 Mr. Brown / enthusiastic / get frustrated with us

→ _____

2 Mrs. Swan / kind / get angry with us

→ _____

3 Ms. Cooper / friendly / forget our birthdays

→ _____

4 Mr. Walker / cheerful / discourage us

→ _____

C Look at the example and complete the sentences.

1 (she / my math scores improve)

→ **Because of her,** my math scores **improved**.

2 (she / I become interested in society)

→ _____

3 (he / I learn to play the guitar)

→ _____

D Look at the pictures. Complete the sentences with the words in the box.

social studies	~~math~~	music

1 She _____ **made** math fun _____ . (fun)

2 He _____ . (interesting)

3 She _____ . (enjoyable)

E Look at the example and rewrite the sentences.

💡 Add "-er" or minus -y and add "-ier" to most adjectives with 1-2 syllables.
   Add "more" to longer adjectives. Some adjectives are irregular, such as good → better.

1 Math is easy.   → Math is **easier than other subjects**.

2 P.E. is exciting.   → _____

3 Music is interesting. → _____

Sentence Practice

A **Read the short paragraph. Correct the mistakes and rewrite the sentences.**

I always thought social studies <u>is</u> dull. But Mr. Walker was cheerful and never <u>discouraging</u> us. He made social studies <u>interestingly</u>. Social studies is <u>important</u> than other subjects.

↓

_____

_____

_____

_____

B **Look at the picture and read the conditions. Write about your favorite teacher like A above.**

Conditions

① Write four sentences.

② Include the following information:
English – boring / Ms. Swan – kind / get angry with us / fun / interesting.

③ Include "make + object + adjective" and a comparative adjective.

_____

_____

_____

_____

Brainstorming

Write about your favorite teacher. Complete the graphic organizer. Use the ideas in Collecting Ideas or come up with your own.

Thank You, _____	
Who	
Appearance	• •
Personality	• •
Why I Am Thankful	• → → •

• **More Subjects**

   history / geography / Korean / art / chemistry / biology

• **More Adjectives**

   complicated / frustrating / boring / hard / exhausting

First Draft

Complete the first draft by using the graphic organizer.

Title _____

Introduction

Dear _____,

Body

Who Do you remember _____? _____ was our

Appearance _____ teacher. _____ was _____

_____. _____ had _____

_____. _____ taught us _____.

I always thought _____ was _____. But

Personality _____ was _____ and _____

Why I Am Thankful _____. Because of _____, _____

_____. _____

made _____! Now, we are _____.

_____ is _____ than other subjects.

I really want to thank _____ for teaching us.

Conclusion

Your friend,

_____

Unit 5

Follow the Rules

Writing Goal	Write about the rules at a public place.
Type of Writing	Expository Writing 〉 Report
	Expository writing gives information about a topic or tells you how to do something.

Before You Write

A **Read and answer the questions.**

1 Where do you like to go on the weekend?

I like to go to _____ .

2 What should you do at the library?

We should _____ .

3 Does your school have many rules?

☐ Yes, it does.   ☐ No, it doesn't.

B **Match the pictures with the correct phrases in the box.**

clean up   be careful   talk quietly
warm up   don't run   turn off your cell phone

1

_____

2

_____

3

_____

4

_____

5

_____

6

_____

Understanding the Model Text

A   **Read the model text and answer the question.**

Rules at the Library

Libraries have some important rules. When you go to the library, you should remember them. First, you should not make noise. Before you go into the library, turn off your cell phone. Talk quietly inside the library. Second, keep the library clean and safe. Don't bring food or drinks inside. You should not bring pets inside, either. Third, be careful with the books. You should not fold or rip the pages. You can make the library a great place. Just follow these rules!

Q   What is the passage mainly about?
a. how to borrow a book
b. how to act at the library

B   **Read the model text again and complete the graphic organizer.**

Rules at the Library	
First	• should not _____ - _____ your cell phone - talk _____
Second	• keep the library _____ - don't _____ or drinks - should not _____
Third	• be careful with the books - _____ or rip the pages

C **Complete the paragraph by using the model text.**

Title	Rules at the Library

Introduction

_____ have some important rules. When you go to the

_____, you should remember them.

Body

First

First, you should _____. Before you

_____, _____.

Second

_____. Second, keep _____

_____. Don't _____.

Third

You should _____. Third, be _____

_____. You should _____

_____.

Conclusion

You can make the _____ a great place. Just follow these

rules!

Collecting Ideas

Look at the example. Fill in the blanks with the phrases in the box.

run on the wet floor   ~~rip the pages~~   make a big mess
don't talk   don't feed the animals   don't run in the hallways

1
library

- talk quietly inside the library
- don't bring food or drinks inside
- should not fold or
  ___rip the pages___

2
movie theater

- _____
  during the movie
- don't throw food on the floor
- should not kick the chair in front of you

3
swimming pool

- stretch your arms and legs
- don't _____
- should not push other swimmers

4
restaurant

- don't shout in the restaurant
- don't _____
- should say please and thank you to the waiters

5
school

- _____
- don't fight with your classmates
- should listen to your teacher

6
pet café

- control your pet in the café
- _____ too much
- should pet the animals gently

54

Sentence Practice

A **Look at the example and complete the sentences.**

1 make noise (X)

→ **First, you should not** make noise. _____

2 be noisy (X)

→ _____

3 get ready to swim (O)

→ _____

4 be quiet (O)

→ _____

Your Idea

5 _____

B **Look at the pictures and complete the sentences.**

💡 When "before" is used as a conjunction, it is followed by a subject and a verb.

1  (turn off your cell phone)

Before you go into the library, turn off your cell phone. _____

2  (warm up)

_____

3  (lower your voice)

_____

4  (help your pet calm down)

_____

5 Your Idea _____

C Look at the example and rewrite the sentences.

> You should be careful with the books.
> → **Be careful with the books.**

1 You should be considerate of other people.

→ _____

2 You should be nice to your teachers.

→ _____

3 You should be polite in the restaurant.

→ _____

D Look at the example and complete the sentences.

💡 Put "don't" before a verb to make a sentence negative.

1 bring food or drinks inside   → **Don't** bring food or drinks inside. _____

2 throw food on the floor   → _____

3 make a big mess   → _____

E Look at the pictures. Complete the sentences with the phrases in the box.

fold or rip the pages   kick the chair in front of you   push other swimmers

1
You should not fold or rip the pages. _____

2
_____

3
_____

Sentence Practice Plus

A **Read the short paragraph. Correct the mistakes and rewrite the sentences.**

Swimming pools have some important rules. First, you <u>should not</u> get ready to swim. Before you <u>going</u> into the pool, warm up. <u>Do</u> run on the wet floor.

_____

_____

_____

_____

B **Look at the picture and read the conditions. Write about the rules at a restaurant like A above.**

Conditions

① Write four sentences.

② Include the following information: make noise / lower your voice / make a big mess.

③ Include "should not" and "before + subject + verb."

_____

_____

_____

_____

Brainstorming

Write about the rules at a public place. Complete the graphic organizer. Use the ideas in Collecting Ideas or come up with your own.

Rules _____	
First	• – –
Second	• – –
Third	• –

● **More Public Places**

hospital / nursing home / supermarket / department store / academy / train station / zoo

First Draft

Complete the first draft by using the graphic organizer.

Title _____

Introduction _____ have some important rules. When you go to

_____, you should remember them.

Body

First   First, you should _____. Before you

_____, _____.

Second   _____. Second, keep

_____. _____.

You should _____.

Third   Third, _____.

You should _____.

Conclusion

You can make the _____ a great place. Just follow

these rules!

Unit 6

A Famous Food

Before You Write

A **Read and answer the questions.**

1 What is your favorite food?

I like _____ .

2 What is a famous food from your country?

_____ is / are famous in my country.

3 What food do you want to try?

I want to try _____ .

B **Match the pictures with the correct words in the box.**

> gimbap / Korea   poutine / Canada   taco / Mexico
> paella / Spain   mochi / Japan   cinnamon roll / Sweden

1

_____

2

_____

3

_____

4

_____

5

_____

6

_____

Understanding the Model Text

A Read the model text and answer the question.

Try Some Poutine!

Do you like cheese and French fries? You should try poutine. It is a famous food in Canada. Poutine is made with French fries, cheese, and gravy. It looks messy but tastes great. You can buy it at a restaurant or a food truck. Some restaurants add other toppings. You can try bacon, turkey, mushrooms, or avocado on top. People usually eat poutine as a meal. Children love to have it for lunch or dinner.

If you visit Canada, you should order some poutine!

Q The concluding sentence is the final thought of the passage. Underline the concluding sentence.

B Read the model text again and complete the graphic organizer.

Poutine	
Where It Is from	a famous food _____
Ingredients and Taste	• made with _____ • looks _____ but tastes _____ • other _____: bacon, turkey, mushrooms, or avocado
Where You Can Buy It	at a restaurant or _____
How to Eat It	• eat poutine as _____ • children: have it for _____

C **Complete the paragraph by using the model text.**

Try Some Poutine!

Do you like _____? You should try

_____.

Where It Is from

_____ a famous food in _____. _____

Ingredients and Taste

made _____.

Where You Can Buy It

It looks _____. You can buy _____

_____. Some restaurants _____

_____. You can try _____

How to Eat It

_____. People usually eat _____

_____. _____ love to have _____

_____.

If you visit _____, you should _____!

Collecting Ideas

Look at the example. Fill in the blanks with the phrases in the box.

~~French fries, cheese~~	rice, seaweed	food coloring
sugar, and cinnamon	meat, and vegetables	rice, shrimp

1

- poutine
- _French fries, cheese_ , and gravy
- looks messy but tastes great

2

- gimbap
- _____, vegetables, and crab
- looks delicious and tastes amazing

3

- cinnamon rolls
- dough, _____
- smell delicious and taste sweet

4

- paella
- _____, meat, and saffron
- looks colorful and tastes delicious

5

- mochi
- rice paste and _____
- looks colorful and tastes sweet

6

- tacos
- tortillas, _____
- smell salty but taste amazing

Sentence Practice

A **Look at the example and complete the sentences.**

1 | cheese / French fries |

→ **Do you like** cheese **and** French fries**?**

2 | rice / seaweed |

→ _____

3 | sweet pastries / cinnamon |

→ _____

4 | desserts / colorful sweets |

→ _____

B **Look at the pictures and complete the sentences.**

| ~~French fries / cheese / gravy~~   dough / sugar / cinnamon |
| tortillas / meat / vegetables   rice / seaweed / vegetables / crab |

💡When the food is uncountable, use "is." When the food is countable, use "are."

1 Poutine **is made with** French fries, cheese, **and** gravy _____ .

2 Gimbap _____ .

3 Cinnamon rolls _____ .

4 Tacos _____ .

5 Your Idea _____

C Look at the example and complete the sentences.

💡Use "but" when one thought is negative and the other is positive.

1 (it / look messy / taste great)

→ It **looks** messy **but tastes** great.

2 (it / look delicious / taste amazing)

→ _____

3 (they / smell salty / taste amazing)

→ _____

D Look at the example and complete the sentences. Change the food to *it* or *them*.

1 children / poutine / for lunch or dinner

→ Children **love to have it** for lunch or dinner.

2 children / gimbap / for lunch or as a snack

→ _____

3 adults / cinnamon rolls / for breakfast with coffee

→ _____

E Look at the pictures and complete the sentences.

1

If you visit Canada, **you should order some** poutine.

2

_____

3

_____

Sentence Practice Plus

A **Read the short paragraph. Correct the mistakes and rewrite the sentences.**

Cinnamon rolls are a famous food <u>at</u> Sweden. They are made <u>in</u> dough, sugar, and cinnamon. They <u>smells</u> delicious and taste sweet. If you visit Sweden, you <u>will</u> order some cinnamon rolls.

_____

_____

_____

_____

B **Look at the picture and read the conditions. Write about tacos like A above.**

Conditions

① Write four sentences.

② Include the following information: tortillas, meat, and vegetables / smell salty – taste amazing.

③ Include "If + subject + verb, you should ~."

_____

_____

_____

_____

Brainstorming

Write about a famous food. Complete the graphic organizer. Use the ideas in Collecting Ideas or come up with your own.

Try Some _____ !	
Where It Is / They Are from	
Ingredients and Taste	• • •
Where You Can Buy It / Them	
How to Eat It / Them	• •

• **More Famous Foods**

Italy – spaghetti / the U.S. – brownies / Vietnam – pho / Korea – bean paste soup / India – samosas

• **More Places to Eat**

food court / convenience store / café / school cafeteria / stadium / fair

First Draft

Complete the first draft by using the graphic organizer.

Title _____

Introduction

Do you like _____? You should try

_____.

Body

Where It Is /
They Are from   _____ a famous food in _____. _____.

Ingredients and
Taste   made _____.

_____. You can buy

Where You Can Buy   _____. Some _____
It / Them

_____. You can try _____

How to Eat It /   _____. People usually eat _____
Them

_____. _____ love to have _____

_____.

Conclusion

If you visit _____, you should order _____!

Unit 7

The Best Place in My Town

Writing Goal	Write about the best place in your town.
Type of Writing	Descriptive Writing Blog

Descriptive writing describes a person, place, or thing. It shows what the person, location, or object is like.

Before You Write

A **Read and answer the questions.**

1 Is there a mountain or a beach in your town?

☐ Yes, there is.   ☐ No, there isn't.

2 What is your favorite place in your town?

My favorite place is _____.

3 Where do you like to go in summer?

I like to go to _____ in summer.

B **Match the pictures with the correct words in the box.**

beach	mountain	art gallery
park	amusement park	farm

1

_____

2

_____

3

_____

4

_____

5

_____

6

_____

Understanding the Model Text

A Read the model text and answer the question.

Crystal Mountain

My town is small, but it has a huge mountain. I like to visit Crystal Mountain in the winter. There are many things to do there. You can go skiing or take a snowboarding class. You can also enter an ice sculpture contest. There is a pond for ice skating, too. If you get hungry, there are a lot of foods to eat. Try some hot soup at a restaurant. Why don't you visit Crystal Mountain with your friends? You will have a fantastic time!

Q What is the passage mainly about?
   a. foods at Crystal Mountain
   b. reasons to visit Crystal Mountain

B Read the model text again and complete the graphic organizer.

Crystal Mountain	
The Place	• What It Is: a huge _____ • When to Visit: in the winter
Things to Do	Activities: • go skiing or _____ • enter _____ Features: • a pond for _____
Foods to Try	some _____ at a restaurant
What You Should Do	• visit Crystal Mountain with _____ → will have _____

C **Complete the paragraph by using the model text.**

Crystal Mountain

Introduction

The Place

My town is _____, _____ it has _____

_____.

Body

When to Visit

I like to visit _____ in the _____.

Things to Do

There are many _____ there. You can

_____. You can also

_____. There _____

_____. If you get _____,

Foods to Try

there are _____. Try _____

_____.

Conclusion

What You Should Do

Why don't you visit _____ with your _____?

You will have _____!

Collecting Ideas

Look at the example. Fill in the blanks with the phrases in the box.

go skiing	feed the goats	try some fresh seafood
try some cotton candy	take a painting class	try some sandwiches

1

- Crystal Mountain
- ___go skiing___

  or take a snowboarding class
- try some hot soup at a restaurant

2

- Green Park
- ride your bike or play tennis
- _____

  and hot dogs at a café

3

- Stone Beach
- swim in the ocean or rent a boat
- _____

  at a restaurant

4

- Ridge Farm
- pick apples or

  _____
- try some apple pie at a food stand

5

- Smith Art Gallery
- see the artwork or

  _____
- try some hot chocolate at a café

6

- Happy Amusement Park
- play games or go on rides
- _____

  at a snack stall

Sentence Practice

A **Look at the example and complete the sentences.**

1 small / but / huge mountain

→ **My town is** small, but **it has a** huge mountain.

2 small / but / beautiful park

→ _____

3 big / and / wonderful art gallery

→ _____

4 big / and / exciting amusement park

→ _____

Your Idea

5 _____

B **Look at the pictures. Complete the sentences with the phrases in the box.**

pick apples   ~~go skiing~~   swim in the ocean   ride your bike

1 (take a snowboarding class)

→ **You can** go skiing **or** take a snowboarding class. _____

2 (rent a boat)

→ _____

3 (play tennis)

→ _____

4 (feed the goats)

→ _____

C Look at the example and rewrite the sentences.

A "to-infinitive" can act as an adjective by modifying a noun.

1 There are many things. You do them there.

→ There are many things **to do** there.

2 There are many snacks. You eat them.

→ _____

3 There are many activities. You do them there.

→ _____

D Look at the example and complete the sentences.

1 (hot soup / restaurant)

→ **Try some** hot soup **at a** restaurant.

2 (fresh seafood / restaurant)

→ _____

3 (sandwiches and hotdogs / café)

→ _____

E Look at the example and rewrite the sentences.

Use "why don't you + verb ~?" to make a suggestion.

1 You should visit Crystal Mountain. You should go with your friends.

→ **Why don't you** visit Crystal Mountain **with** your friends**?**

2 You should visit Green Park. You should go with your friends.

→ _____

3 You should visit Ridge Farm. You should go with your parents.

→ _____

Sentence Practice Plus

A **Read the short paragraph. Correct the mistakes and rewrite the sentences.**

My town is small, <u>so</u> it has a sandy beach.

You can <u>swimming</u> in the ocean or rent a boat.

If you get hungry, there are many foods <u>eat</u>.

Why <u>do</u> you visit Stone Beach with your family?

_____

_____

_____

_____

B **Look at the picture and read the conditions. Write about Ridge Farm like A above.**

Conditions

① Write four sentences.

② Include the following information:
small – amazing / pick apples, feed the goats / many snacks – eat / your parents.

③ Include a "to-infinitive as an adjective" and "why don't you + verb ~?"

_____

_____

_____

_____

Brainstorming

Write about the best place in your town. Complete the graphic organizer. Use the ideas in Collecting Ideas or come up with your own.

The Place	• What It Is: • When to Visit:
Things to Do	Activities: • • Features: •
Foods to Try	
What You Should Do	• →

◆ **More Activities**

the beach – enter a sandcastle contest / the farm – ride a horse /
the art gallery – meet some artists / the amusement park – watch a show

First Draft

Complete the first draft by using the graphic organizer.

Title	_____

Introduction
The Place

My town is _____, _____ it has _____

_____.

Body

When to Visit

I like to visit _____ in the _____.

Things to Do

There are _____. You can

_____. You can also

_____. There

_____. If you

Foods to Try

get hungry, there _____.

Try _____.

Conclusion

What You Should Do

Why don't you visit _____ with your

_____? You will have _____!

Unit 8

My Favorite Movie

Writing Goal	Write about your favorite movie.
Type of Writing	Expository Writing » Movie Review
	Expository writing gives information about a topic or tells you how to do something.

Before You Write

A **Read and answer the questions.**

1 Do you enjoy watching movies?

☐ Yes, I do. ☐ No, I don't.

2 What is your favorite movie?

My favorite movie is _____ .

3 Who is the main character of the movie?

The main character is _____ .

B **Fill in the chart with the words in the box.**

beast	village	dragon	castle
thief	magic school	witch	tower

Settings	Characters
• _____	• _____
• _____	• _____
• _____	• _____
• _____	• _____

Understanding the Model Text

A **Read the model text and answer the question.**

> ### My Favorite Movie: *Tangled*
>
> I enjoy watching movies. My favorite is *Tangled*. It is one of the most popular children's movies. The main character is Rapunzel. She has magic hair. She lives in a tall tower. She wants to go outside and have an adventure. One day, a thief helps Rapunzel run away. A witch tries to catch her. She wants Rapunzel's magic hair. Rapunzel defeats the witch with her friends. In the end, she meets her real parents. I think the end is very touching.

Q The concluding sentence is the final thought of the passage. Underline the concluding sentence.

B **Read the model text again and complete the graphic organizer.**

Tangled	
The Main Character: _____	• has _____ • lives in _____ • wants to go outside and _____
The Plot	• One day: a thief helps Rapunzel _____ • _____ tries to catch her - wants Rapunzel's hair • Rapunzel _____ with her friends • In the end: Rapunzel meets _____
My Opinion	the end is _____

C **Complete the paragraph by using the model text.**

| Title | My Favorite Movie: *Tangled* |

Introduction

I _____ movies. My favorite is _____.

It is one of _____ children's movies.

Body

The Main Character The main character is _____. She _____.

She lives _____. She wants to _____

The Plot _____. One day, _____

_____. _____.

_____.

_____.

In the end, _____.

Conclusion

My Opinion I think _____.

Collecting Ideas

Look at the example. Fill in the blanks with the phrases in the box.

~~wants to go outside~~	favorite toy	learn magic
ride the dragon	his neighborhood safe	save her father

1

Tangled

- Rapunzel
- _____wants to go outside_____ and have an adventure
- defeats the witch with her friends

2

How to Train Your Dragon

- Hiccup
- wants to impress his strong father and kill a dragon
- learns to _____

3

Beauty and the Beast

- Belle
- is always bored and wants to have an adventure
- goes to _____

4

Toy Story

- Woody
- wants to be Andy's _____
- rescues Buzz from a mean boy

5

Harry Potter and the Sorcerer's Stone

- Harry
- is lonely and wants to _____
- looks for the sorcerer's stone

6

Spiderman: Homecoming

- Peter
- wants to keep _____
- fights the evil Vulture

Sentence Practice

A **Look at the example and complete the sentences.**

(enjoy / watch / movies)
→ I enjoy **watching** movies.

1 (love / watch / movies)

→ _____

2 (really like / watch / films)

→ _____

3 (enjoy / watch / animation)

→ _____

Your Idea

4 _____

B **Look at the example and complete the sentences.**

Add "-est" to the end of an adjective to make the superlative form.
Place "most" before adjectives with three or more syllables.

1 popular

→ **It is one of the most** popular **children's movies**. _____

2 funny

→ _____

3 exciting

→ _____

4 sad

→ _____

Your Idea

5 _____

C **Read the plot of *How to Train Your Dragon* and complete the sentences.**

~~main character~~	one day	impress his strong father
In the end	ride the dragon	very kind

1 The _____main character_____ is Hiccup.

2 He wants to _____ and kill a dragon.

3 _____, Hiccup catches a dragon.

4 The dragon is _____.

5 Hiccup learns to _____.

6 _____, his village stops killing dragons.

D **Read the plot of *Spiderman: Homecoming* and write the sentences.**

~~He wants to keep his neighborhood safe.~~	Peter fights the evil Vulture.
In the end, Peter saves his neighborhood.	One day, Peter meets the Vulture.

1 The main character is Peter.

2 He wants to keep his neighborhood safe.

3 _____

4 The Vulture wants to sell dangerous weapons.

5 _____

6 _____

Sentence Practice ^{Plus}

A **Read the short paragraph. Correct the mistakes and rewrite the sentences.**

I enjoy <u>watch</u> movies. My favorite is *Beauty and the Beast*. It is one of the <u>exciting</u> children's movies. One day, Belle's father <u>go</u> to a castle. An evil beast catches him. <u>On</u> the end, the beast becomes a kind prince.

_____

_____

_____

_____

B **Look at the picture and read the conditions. Write about *Harry Potter and the Sorcerer's Stone* like A above.**

Conditions

① Write six sentences.

② Include the following information: enjoy – watch / cool / Harry – get invited to a magic school / Hogwarts – so wonderful / Harry – save the school.

③ Include "enjoy + verb-ing" and "one of the + superlative adjective."

_____

_____

_____

_____

Brainstorming

Write about your favorite movie. Complete the graphic organizer. Use the ideas in Collecting Ideas or come up with your own.

My Favorite Movie: _____	
The Main Character: _____	• • •
The Plot	• One day: • — • • In the end:
My Opinion	

• **More Movies and Main Characters**

Iron Man –Tony Stark / *Frozen* – Anna / *Moana* – Moana / *Kung Fu Panda* – Po / *Home Alone* - Kevin

• **More Adjectives**

thrilling / funny / entertaining / heartwarming / impressive

First Draft

Complete the first draft by using the graphic organizer.

Title _____

Introduction

I _____. My favorite is _____

_____. It is one of _____ children's

movies.

Body

The Main Character

The main character is _____. _____

_____. _____ lives _____.

The Plot

_____.

One day, _____.

_____.

_____.

_____.

In the end, _____.

Conclusion

My Opinion

I think _____.

Vocabulary & Structure Review

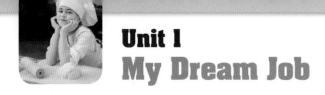

Unit 1
My Dream Job

Read the words and phrases. Write the meaning next to each word and phrase.

1	pilot		11	medical school	
2	grow up		12	florist	
3	travel (*v.*)		13	animator	
4	visit		14	animated films	
5	country		15	cartoon	
6	responsible		16	cure (*v.*)	
7	difficult		17	patient (*a., n.*)	
8	prepare		18	architect	
9	flight school		19	vet (= veterinarian)	
10	hardworking		20	take care of	

Structures

1 when + subject + verb

> e.g I want to be a pilot <u>when I grow</u> up.
>
> I will visit many countries <u>when I am</u> a pilot.

2 because + subject + verb

> e.g I like this job <u>because I love</u> to travel.

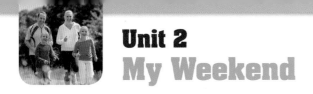

Unit 2
My Weekend

Read the words and phrases. Write the meaning next to each word and phrase.

1	exciting		11	wake up (= get up)	
2	weekend		12	brush one's teeth	
3	often		13	take a shower	
4	always		14	get dressed	
5	sometimes		15	go shopping	
6	grocery		16	ride a bike	
7	swimming pool		17	go for a walk	
8	breakfast		18	go out for dinner	
9	playground		19	all day	
10	a lot of (= many, much)		20	get some rest	

Structures

1 adverbs of frequency: always, usually, often, sometimes, etc.

  e.g I <u>usually</u> get up late.

     In the evening, we <u>often</u> go out for dinner.

2 after + noun / after + subject + verb

  e.g <u>After lunch</u>, I watch my favorite TV program.

     <u>After I wake up</u>, I make breakfast with my dad.

Unit 3
My Special Birthday Gift

Read the words and phrases. Write the meaning next to each word and phrase.

1	birthday		11	warm	
2	open (v.) (opened-opened)		12	scarf	
3	special		13	polka dot	
4	gift		14	model car	
5	inside (prep.)		15	stripe	
6	bracelet		16	spot	
7	heart		17	spaceship	
8	think (thought-thought)		18	cell phone case	
9	lose (lost-lost)		19	remind A of B	
10	wear		20	write in one's diary	

1 the past tense

> e.g I <u>opened</u> the box and <u>saw</u> a beautiful bracelet.
> I <u>thought</u> it <u>was</u> so pretty!

2 give + indirect object + direct object

> e.g Last year, my best friend <u>gave me a special gift</u>.

Unit 4
My Favorite Teacher

Read the words and phrases. Write the meaning next to each word and phrase.

1	grade		11	improve	
2	thin (← fat)		12	subject	
3	curly (*a.*)		13	thank (*v.*)	
4	freckle		14	skill	
5	teach (taught-taught)		15	enthusiastic	
6	math (= mathematics)		16	friendly (= kind)	
7	never		17	cheerful	
8	scold		18	discourage	
9	because of		19	enjoyable	
10	score (*n.*)		20	dull (= boring)	

1 make + object + adjective

e.g She <u>made math fun</u>!

2 comparative adjectives

e.g Math is <u>easier than</u> other subjects.

P.E. is <u>more exciting than</u> other subjects.

Unit 5
Follow the Rules

Words & Phrases

Read the words and phrases. Write the meaning next to each word and phrase.

1	rule (*n.*)		11	follow	
2	important		12	kick	
3	quietly		13	wet (↔ dry)	
4	safe		14	hallway	
5	drink (*n.*)		15	gently	
6	pet (*n., v.*)		16	considerate	
7	either		17	turn off (↔ turn on)	
8	careful		18	make noise	
9	fold		19	make a mess	
10	rip		20	calm down	

Structures

1 should (not)

e.g You <u>should not</u> make noise.

You <u>should</u> listen to your teacher.

2 before + subject + verb

e.g <u>Before you go</u> into the library, turn off your cell phone.

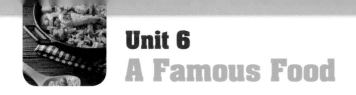

Unit 6
A Famous Food

Read the words and phrases. Write the meaning next to each word and phrase.

1	French fries		11	mushroom	
2	try (*v.*)		12	meal	
3	famous		13	order (*v.*)	
4	gravy (*n.*)		14	seaweed	
5	messy		15	dough	
6	taste (*v.*)		16	cinnamon	
7	add		17	meat	
8	topping		18	sweets	
9	salty		19	be made with	
10	turkey		20	food coloring	

Structures

1 look / smell / taste + adjective

e.g It <u>looks messy</u> but <u>tastes great</u>.

2 If + subject + verb, you should ~

e.g <u>If you visit</u> Canada, <u>you should</u> order some poutine!

Unit 7
The Best Place in My Town

Words & Phrases

Read the words and phrases. Write the meaning next to each word and phrase.

1	town		11	ocean	
2	huge		12	rent	
3	thing		13	pick	
4	enter		14	seafood	
5	sculpture		15	snack stall (= food stand)	
6	contest		16	go on rides	
7	snowboarding		17	go skiing	
8	fantastic		18	take a class	
9	artwork		19	cotton candy	
10	sandy		20	amusement park	

Structures

1 **to-infinitive as an adjective**

e.g There are many things <u>to do</u> there.

2 **Why don't you + verb ~?**

e.g <u>Why don't you visit</u> Crystal Mountain with your friends?

Unit 8
My Favorite Movie

Read the words and phrases. Write the meaning next to each word and phrase.

1	enjoy		11	real	
2	popular		12	touching	
3	main character		13	neighborhood	
4	magic (*a.*)		14	evil (*a.*)	
5	tower		15	mean (*a.*)	
6	adventure		16	beast	
7	thief		17	rescue (= save)	
8	witch		18	impress	
9	catch		19	run away	
10	defeat (*v.*)		20	in the end	

Structures

1 gerund as an object: enjoy + verb-ing

  e.g I <u>enjoy watching</u> movies.

2 one of the + superlative adjective

  e.g It is <u>one of the most popular</u> movies.

Memo

Memo

Memo

Memo

Essential Guide to Writing
Writing Avenue

Workbook

Paragraph Writing

2

DARAKWON

Essential Guide to Writing

Writing Avenue

Workbook

Paragraph Writing

2

DARAKWON

Unit 1 My Dream Job

Ⓐ Look at the example and complete the sentences.

1 ┌─────────────┐
     │ love to travel │
     └─────────────┘

   → **I like this job because I** love to travel. _____

2 ┌────────────────────┐
     │ like to help sick people │
     └────────────────────┘

   → _____

3 ┌────────────────┐
     │ like to grow flowers │
     └────────────────┘

   → _____

4 ┌──────────────────┐
     │ love to draw cartoons │
     └──────────────────┘

   → _____

Ⓑ Look at the example and complete the sentences.

1 (visit many countries / pilot)

   → **I will** visit many countries **when I am a** pilot. _____

2 (cure many patients / doctor)

   → _____

3 (make beautiful flower bouquets / florist)

   → _____

4 (work on animated films / animator)

   → _____

2

C **Match the phrases. Then, write the sentences.**

1	I want to be	•	•	when I am a pilot
2	I think I will be a	•	•	so I need to prepare
3	Pilots need to be smart	•	•	and responsible
4	They fly the planes	•	•	and study hard
5	They also need to	•	•	great pilot someday
6	It is a difficult job,	•	•	a pilot when I grow up
7	I will go to a flight school	•	•	know a lot about airplanes
8	I will visit many countries	•	•	from one place to another

1 _____

2 _____

3 _____

4 _____

5 _____

6 _____

7 _____

8 _____

Revise & Edit

Write about your dream job. Refer to the First Draft in the student book. Then, edit your paragraph.

Title	
Introduction	
Body	
Conclusion	

Editing Checklist ☐ Capitalization   ☐ Punctuation   ☐ Grammar   ☐ Spelling

Final Draft

Write the final draft.

Title

Unit 2 My Weekend

(A) Look at the example and complete the sentences.

> always (100%)   usually (90%)
> often (70%)   sometimes (50%)

1 | get up late / 90% |

→ **I usually get up late.** _____

2 | make pancakes / 50% |

→ _____

3 | get up early / 100% |

→ _____

4 | make fresh juice / 70% |

→ _____

(B) Look at the example and complete the sentences.

1 (lunch → watch my favorite TV program)

→ **After** lunch, **I** watch my favorite TV program. ___

2 (lunch → go to the library)

→ _____

3 (lunch → watch music videos on YouTube)

→ _____

4 (dinner → go for a walk)

→ _____

C **Match the phrases. Then, write the sentences.**

1	It takes	•	•	things on the weekend
2	Then we go for	•	•	at the playground
3	I do a lot of fun	•	•	ride our bikes
4	We play soccer and	•	•	breakfast with my dad
5	In the evening,	•	•	grocery shopping
6	After I wake up, I make	•	•	almost all day
7	Then I meet my friends	•	•	we often go out for dinner
8	On Sundays, my family goes	•	•	a walk in the park

1 _____

2 _____

3 _____

4 _____

5 _____

6 _____

7 _____

8 _____

Revise & Edit

Write about what you do on the weekend. Refer to the First Draft in the student book. Then, edit your paragraph.

Title

Introduction

Body

Conclusion

Editing Checklist ☐ Capitalization ☐ Punctuation ☐ Grammar ☐ Spelling

Final Draft

Write the final draft.

| Title | |

Unit 3 My Special Birthday Gift

A **Look at the example and rewrite the sentences. Change the verbs to the past tense.**

1 I open the box and see a beautiful bracelet.

→ I **opened** the box and **saw** a beautiful bracelet.

2 I think it is so pretty.

→ _____

3 It is inside a blue bag.

→ _____

4 I open the bag and see a new diary.

→ _____

B **Look at the example and unscramble the sentences. Change the verbs to the past tense.**

1 (last year, / a special gift / me / my best friend / give)

→ **Last year, my best friend gave me a special gift.**

2 (a special gift / me / my aunt / last year, / give)

→ _____

3 (me / my grandmother / two years ago, / give / a special gift)

→ _____

4 (last year, / me / a special gift / give / my parents)

→ _____

C **Match the phrases. Then, write the sentences.**

1	I wear my	•	• a pink box
2	I thought	•	• it was so pretty
3	It was inside	•	• on April 10
4	I hope I never	•	• colorful hearts on it
5	It is silver with	•	• bracelet every day
6	It reminds me	•	• of my best friend
7	We eat cake together,	•	• lose my special bracelet
8	My birthday is	•	• and then I open gifts

1 _____

2 _____

3 _____

4 _____

5 _____

6 _____

7 _____

8 _____

Revise & Edit

Write about a special birthday gift you received. Refer to the First Draft in the student book. Then, edit your paragraph.

Title	

Introduction

Body

Conclusion

Editing Checklist   ☐ Capitalization   ☐ Punctuation   ☐ Grammar   ☐ Spelling

Final Draft

Write the final draft.

Title

Unit 4 My Favorite Teacher

A **Look at the example and complete the sentences.**

1 | she / math / fun |

→ She **made** math fun. _____

2 | she / English / interesting |

→ _____

3 | he / P.E. / exciting |

→ _____

4 | he / social studies / enjoyable |

→ _____

B **Look at the example and complete the sentences.**

1 (math / easy)

→ Math **is easier than other subjects**. _____

2 (P.E. / exciting)

→ _____

3 (social studies / important)

→ _____

4 (science / good)

→ _____

C **Match the phrases. Then, write the sentences.**

1	Now, we are •	• fourth-grade teacher
2	She taught •	• hair and freckles
3	I always thought •	• math was difficult
4	But Miss Bell was patient •	• in middle school
5	She had curly brown •	• us math
6	She was our •	• and never scolded us
7	Because of her, my •	• Miss Bell for teaching us
8	I really want to thank •	• math scores improved

1 _____

2 _____

3 _____

4 _____

5 _____

6 _____

7 _____

8 _____

Revise & Edit

Write about your favorite teacher. Refer to the First Draft in the student book. Then, edit your paragraph.

Title	

Introduction

Body

Conclusion

Editing Checklist   ☐ Capitalization   ☐ Punctuation   ☐ Grammar   ☐ Spelling

Final Draft

Write the final draft.

Title

Unit 5 **Follow the Rules**

A **Look at the example and complete the sentences.**

1 bring pets inside (X)

→ **You should not** bring pets inside.

2 clean up when the movie is over (O)

→ _____

3 make noise in the restaurant (X)

→ _____

4 pet the animals gently (O)

→ _____

B **Look at the example and complete the sentences.**

1 | library / turn off your cell phone |

→ **Before you go into the** library, turn off your cell phone.

2 | movie theater / lower your voice |

→ _____

3 | swimming pool / warm up |

→ _____

4 | school / slow down and be quiet |

→ _____

18

C **Match the phrases. Then, write the sentences.**

1	Talk quietly	•	• rip the pages
2	Libraries have	•	• or drinks inside
3	You can make	•	• clean and safe
4	First, you should	•	• not make noise
5	Don't bring food	•	• inside the library
6	You should not fold or	•	• you should remember them
7	Second, keep the library	•	• some important rules
8	When you go to the library,	•	• the library a great place

1 _____

2 _____

3 _____

4 _____

5 _____

6 _____

7 _____

8 _____

Revise & Edit

Write about the rules at a public place. Refer to the First Draft in the student book. Then, edit your paragraph.

Title	

Introduction

Body

Conclusion

Editing Checklist ☐ Capitalization ☐ Punctuation ☐ Grammar ☐ Spelling

Final Draft

Write the final draft.

Title

Unit 6 A Famous Food

A **Look at the example and rewrite the sentences with *and* or *but*.**

1   It looks messy. It tastes great.

→ It looks messy **but** tastes great.

2   It looks colorful. It tastes delicious.

→

3   They smell delicious. They taste sweet.

→

4   They smell salty. They taste amazing.

→

B **Look at the example and rewrite the sentences.**

1   You visit Canada. You order some poutine.

→ **If** you visit Canada, you **should** order some poutine.

2   You visit Sweden. You order some cinnamon rolls.

→

3   You visit Mexico. You order some tacos.

→

4   You visit Japan. You order some mochi.

→

C Match the phrases. Then, write the sentences.

1	It is a famous	·	· but tastes great
2	It looks messy	·	· food in Canada
3	You can buy it at	·	· add other toppings
4	Children love to have it	·	· for lunch or dinner
5	Some restaurants	·	· a meal
6	If you visit Canada,	·	· French fries, cheese, and gravy
7	Poutine is made with	·	· you should order some poutine
8	People usually eat poutine as	·	· a restaurant or a food truck

1 _____

2 _____

3 _____

4 _____

5 _____

6 _____

7 _____

8 _____

Revise & Edit

Write about a famous food. Refer to the First Draft in the student book. Then, edit your paragraph.

Title

Introduction

Body

Conclusion

Editing Checklist ☐ Capitalization ☐ Punctuation ☐ Grammar ☐ Spelling

Final Draft

Write the final draft.

Title

Unit 7 The Best Place in My Town

A **Look at the example and complete the sentences.**

1 | many / things / do |

→ **There are** many things **to** do.

2 | many / foods / eat |

→

3 | many / snacks / eat |

→

4 | a lot of / activities / do |

→

B **Look at the example and complete the sentences.**

1 Crystal Mountain / friends

→ **Why don't you visit** Crystal Mountain **with your** friends?

2 the Smith Art Gallery / friends

→

3 Ridge Farm / parents

→

4 Happy Amusement Park / cousins

→

C **Match the phrases. Then, write the sentences.**

1 You will have a   •   • an ice sculpture contest

2 There is a pond   •   • soup at a restaurant

3 You can also enter   •   • for ice skating, too

4 Try some hot   •   • but it has a huge mountain

5 You can go skiing or   •   • there are a lot of foods to eat

6 My town is small,   •   • Crystal Mountain in the winter

7 If you get hungry,   •   • take a snowboarding class

8 I like to visit   •   • fantastic time

1 _____

2 _____

3 _____

4 _____

5 _____

6 _____

7 _____

8 _____

Revise & Edit

Write about the best place in your town. Refer to the First Draft in the student book. Then, edit your paragraph.

Title

Introduction

Body

Conclusion

Editing Checklist   ☐ Capitalization   ☐ Punctuation   ☐ Grammar   ☐ Spelling

Final Draft

Write the final draft.

Title

Unit 8 My Favorite Movie

A **Look at the example and correct the sentences.**

1 | I enjoy watch movies. |

→ I enjoy **watching** movies. _____

2 | I love to watching movies. |

→ _____

3 | I really liking watching films. |

→ _____

4 | I enjoy to watch animation. |

→ _____

B **Look at the example and rewrite the sentences.**

1 (It is a popular children's movie.)

→ It is **one of the most** popular children's **movies**. _____

2 (It is a cool children's movie.)

→ _____

3 (It is an interesting children's movie.)

→ _____

4 (It is a sad children's movie.)

→ _____

C **Match the phrases. Then, write the sentences.**

1	She wants to go outside	•	•	is Rapunzel
2	A witch tries to	•	•	catch her
3	It is one of the	•	•	very touching
4	I think the end is	•	•	her real parents
5	Rapunzel defeats	•	•	and have an adventure
6	The main character	•	•	Rapunzel run away
7	In the end, she meets	•	•	most popular children's movies
8	One day, a thief helps	•	•	the witch with her friends

1 _____

2 _____

3 _____

4 _____

5 _____

6 _____

7 _____

8 _____

Revise & Edit

Write about your favorite movie. Refer to the First Draft in the student book. Then, edit your paragraph.

Title	

Introduction

Body

Conclusion

Editing Checklist ☐ Capitalization ☐ Punctuation ☐ Grammar ☐ Spelling

Final Draft

Write the final draft.

Title

Memo

Memo

Essential Guide to Writing

Writing Avenue

Paragraph Writing